CANTERBURY CATHEDRAL

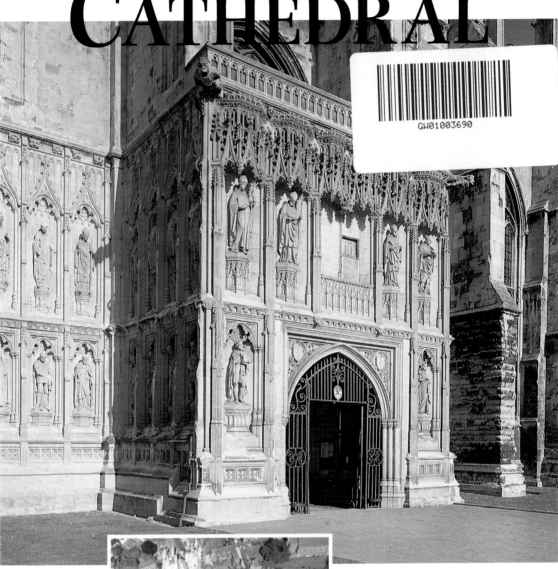

GW01003690

Above:
The south-west porch, the main entrance to the cathedral in daily use.

Right:
Aerial view of Canterbury Cathedral.

Contents

History Chart

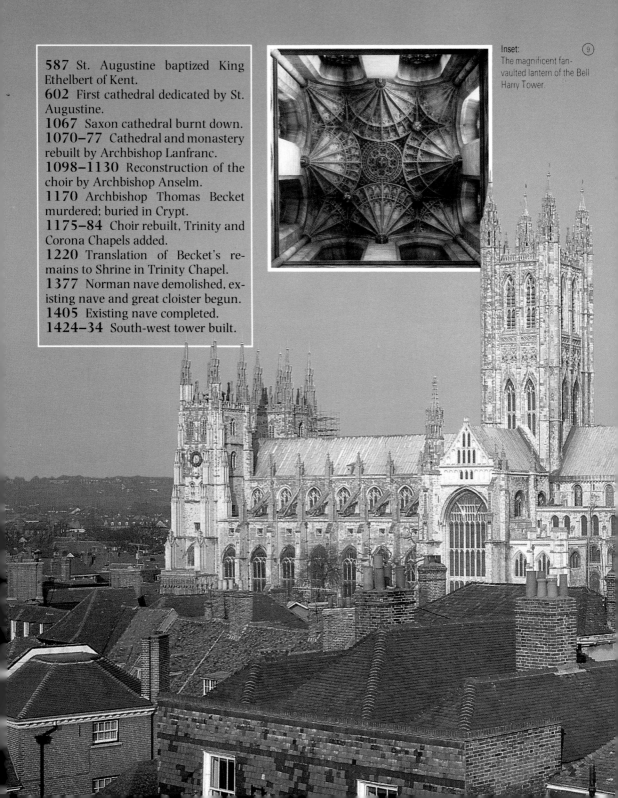

587 St. Augustine baptized King Ethelbert of Kent.
602 First cathedral dedicated by St. Augustine.
1067 Saxon cathedral burnt down.
1070–77 Cathedral and monastery rebuilt by Archbishop Lanfranc.
1098–1130 Reconstruction of the choir by Archbishop Anselm.
1170 Archbishop Thomas Becket murdered; buried in Crypt.
1175–84 Choir rebuilt, Trinity and Corona Chapels added.
1220 Translation of Becket's remains to Shrine in Trinity Chapel.
1377 Norman nave demolished, existing nave and great cloister begun.
1405 Existing nave completed.
1424–34 South-west tower built.

Inset:
The magnificent fan-vaulted lantern of the Bell Harry Tower.

9

*c.*1450 Pulpitum constructed.
1468 West transepts completed.
1494 The Bell Harry tower commissioned by Prior Sellinge.
1517 Christ Church gateway completed.
1538 Becket's Shrine plundered. St. Augustine's Abbey demolished.
1540 Dissolution of Christ Church Priory by Henry VIII.
1541 Royal charter established Dean and Chapter of new cathedral foundation. Henry VIII also granted the King's School a charter.

1642–8 Destruction of monuments, glass, etc., in Civil War.
1660 Cathedral restoration begun.
1682 Completion of choir return stalls.
1832 Replacement of Lanfranc's north-west tower by a copy of the south-west tower.
1844 Archbishop's throne replaced.
1862 South-west porch and tower restored.
1898 Nave pulpit installed.
1954 War damaged library rebuilt.

The Cradle of English Christianity

The supremacy of Canterbury amongst the cathedrals of England is due in large part to the sacrifice of Thomas the Martyr. Without his bloody death in 1170 (of which more later) and his canonisation as a saint in 1173, pilgrims and their money would not have found their way to Canterbury. As it was, the fire that devastated the cathedral in 1174 provided the monks with a marvellous opportunity to reconstruct a magnificent setting for a Shrine of Thomas of Canterbury, Saint and Martyr, whose fame was spreading throughout Christendom.

The Cathedral Church of Christ, Canterbury, of course, existed long before Becket's time. Augustine in 597, on a missionary expedition to convert the heathen English, had made his way to Canterbury, the home of King Ethelbert and his French wife, Bertha. The Venerable Bede, a conscientious historian, tells us: 'There was nearby on the east of the city a church built in ancient times in honour of St. Martin while the Romans were still in Britain, in which the Queen [Bertha] who as has been said was a Christian, used to pray. In this church they first began to meet, to chant the psalms, to pray, to say mass, to preach and to baptize until, when the King had been converted to the faith, they re-

ceived greater liberty to preach every-
where and to build and restore churches.'

In 602 Augustine, who had by then
baptized many English people, was con-
secrated Archbishop of the English. (The
Pope appointed another archbishop at
York.) He had already founded the Ben-
edictine monastery dedicated to St. Peter
and St. Paul, which was later called St.
Augustine's, but now as Archbishop he

needed a cathedral. He chose to stay in
Canterbury, where he was doing well,
rather than go to London, and King
Ethelbert gave him a Roman church to
restore, as Bede tells us. 'After Augustine
had received his episcopal See in the
Royal City [Canterbury] he, with the
help of the King, restored the church in it
which, as he had been informed, had
been built in ancient times by the hands
of Roman believers; he dedicated it in the
name of the Holy Saviour our Lord and
God Jesus Christ, and there he established a dwelling for himself and all his
successors.' Only the name, Christ
Church, remains but our present cathedral is built on its site.

The cradle of English Christianity,
Canterbury, converted the Saxons to
Christ; today, all Anglican churches
through the breadth of the world look to
Canterbury as their spiritual home. Indeed, the first Norman Archbishop, Lanfranc, used his influence with William
the Conqueror to secure the supremacy
of Canterbury over York with the Accord
of Winchester in 1072. In the presence
of William and his queen, Matilda, a

council of bishops subscribed to Canterbury's primacy; Bishop Thomas of York reluctantly added *Concedo*, 'I agree', to his name.

The construction of the magnificent building that we know today as Canterbury Cathedral was severely hampered by fire several times. Very little of the Norman work done by the energetic Archbishop Lanfranc (1070–89), who rebuilt the Saxon cathedral, remains today. His successor, Archbishop Anselm, scholastic and saintly, was responsible for the tremendous crypt and the little staircase towers abutting on the two eastern transepts; there are still traces of contemporary wall painting in St. Gabriel's Chapel. Above the crypt he built a magnificent choir which was to last barely four decades before being destroyed by the great fire of 1174.

The monks determined to rebuild, not only to the glory of God, but to the glory of Thomas Becket. They employed the

great Norman architect, William of Sens, who directed the rebuilding of the choir. Crippled by a fall from the scaffolding, William returned to France and his place was taken by William the Englishman who built the transepts, Trinity Chapel, corona and crypt.

The purpose of the wonderful choir of the two Williams was to hold the Shrine at its eastern end, guarded from the 'Watching Chamber' in the tower of St. Anselm. On 7th July 1220, the Jubilee of the Martyrdom, in the presence of King Henry III and upon the shoulders of the great ecclesiastics in Europe and four of the noblest English lords, the Saint's relics were carried in a chest up the successive stages of the cathedral – one of the features of Canterbury – until they reached the Shrine. That was the first festival-day of the 'Translation of St. Thomas', and it took four successive archbishops after Stephen Langton to pay off the expenses.

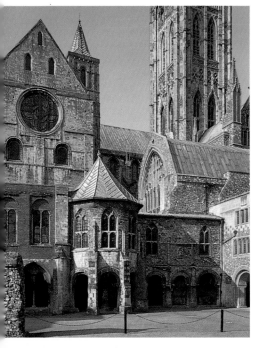

Left: ⑭
The 12th-century Norman water tower built by Prior Wibert as part of a water system is still in use today.

Above: ①
The early 12th-century Chapel of Our Lady Undercroft, famous for its Romanesque pillars, was a favourite chapel of the Black Prince. Above the altar is an 18th-century statue in Portuguese ivory of the Blessed Virgin Mary.

Right:
The cloister, built between 1396 and 1420. The vaulting is adorned with more than 800 medieval coats of arms.

The Murder of Becket

Henry II's challenge 'Not one will deliver me from this low-born priest' as he raged in France against the insubordinate and exasperating Becket, was enough for four of his knights – William de Tracey, Reginald Fitzurse, Richard Brito and Hugh de Morville – who crossed the Channel too quickly to be halted by couriers sent after them. They murdered Becket whilst Vespers was being sung.

All Christendom was appalled, and the emotional reaction was tremendous. Thomas was accounted a saint even before his canonization in 1173: miraculous cures and powers were alleged to exist at his tomb in the crypt; churches and abbeys were founded in his honour

Top left: (17)
A 13th-century stained glass panel, after restoration, from the north aisle of the Trinity Chapel, showing St. Thomas Becket robed and mitred as archbishop.

Centre left: (19)
One of the scenes commemorating the miracles of St. Thomas in the early 13th-century windows of the Trinity Chapel.

Bottom left: (19)
St. Thomas appears to William of Kellett in a dream. A scene from the miracle window in the south aisle of the Trinity Chapel.

Right: (11)
This panel, hanging in the north choir aisle, is a copy of a medieval painting of the martyrdom of St. Thomas Becket. The original, much defaced, hangs at the head of the tomb of King Henry IV in the Trinity Chapel.

It is unlikely that we shall ever know with any certainty what it was about the character of Thomas Becket that led him to be regarded as saintly by his household and 'our traitor' by Henry II. Undoubtedly he was a proud, forceful character who surrounded himself with many servants whilst showing great humility in works of charity.

in various parts of Europe; children and bells were christened Thomas; statues were made and windows executed to his praise and multitudes flocked to Canterbury to the two hallowed spots – the site of the murder and the place of his tomb.

Two months before the great fire of 1174 the King himself had set an example. Under the gaze of the people of Canterbury, on the 12th July, the proud-tempered Henry walked barefoot and penitent from the west of the city to the cathedral. Awaiting him in the crypt were prior, bishops and monks and

'Regale of France' – the most splendid ornament the Shrine was ever to have, said to be the finest jewel in Europe, a king's, indeed a kingdom's, ransom.

For 350 years Canterbury was to be one of Christendom's chief places of pilgrimage, surpassed perhaps only by Jerusalem and Rome.

Above: ⑥

This modern sculpture, dedicated in 1986, marks the scene of Becket's murder in the north-west transept, known as the Martyrdom.

Left: ⑲

Three mailed knights at the cathedral door, c.1220, are part of a series of windows in the Trinity Chapel depicting the murder of Thomas Becket.

there, on his knees at the tomb, the King of England endured the scourging of the clerics, there he performed an all-night vigil and thence he continued his way to London.

Within a generation his two sons would also come – Richard Lionheart, from his landing at Sandwich, to give thanks to God and St. Thomas for safe deliverance; and John in splendid state from his coronation. But, very soon after their father's visit, there had come in 1179 the first King of France ever to set foot in England, Louis VII, to plead for his son's recovery from illness through the mediation of St. Thomas.

A whole night Louis spent in prayer at the tomb and upon it he placed rich offerings including the famous jewel, the

. . . from every shires end
Of Engelond, to Caunterbury they wende.

CROYD

FARNHAM   GUILDFORD   RE

ALTON   DORKING

ALRESFORD

WINCHESTER

One of the best-known pilgrim routes to Canterbury was along the North Downs from Winchester – still known as The Pilgrims Way.

RIVER THAMES

CHATHAM

ROCHESTER

SEVENOAKS

RIVER MEDWAY

CANTERBURY

Opposite: ⑨
The choir, looking east.

Left: ㉚
These four panels from the bottom left-hand corner of the 12th-century south-west transept window show Old Testament figures. The royal arms above the figures are of a later date.

Below left: ⑩
Erected by Prior Chillenden in about 1400, this carved stone pulpitum separates the choir from the nave.

Below right: ㉔
St. Paul, shaking off the viper at Melita, is depicted on a 12th-century mural in St. Anselm's Chapel.

The Shrine of St. Thomas

The City prospered. 'This Citie hath been chiefly maintained by two things,' wrote the Protestant Lambarde. 'First, by the residence and Hospitalitie of the Archbishop and Religious persons, and then by the liberalitie and expense of such as either gadded to St. Thomas for help and devotion, or travelled towards the Sea side for their private affairs and business.'

City officialdom, interested in trade, afforded police protection. 'No innkeeper or host,' ran one of their bye-laws, 'when any Pilgrims or strangers come to the City, shall catch them by their reins, their clothing or their Staves and try to make them come into his Inn, nor shall any cross over the thresholds of his Inn when shouting at the said Pilgrims and strangers passing along, inviting him in, under pain of imprisonment or fine.'

Pilgrims came from foreign parts and the west country, but the greatest throngs of all would come from London; like the band of twenty-nine immortalized by Geoffrey Chaucer. They found lodging in inns, convents and hospitals. Others would lodge in the precincts and these would enter by the Almonry Yard (better known as the Mint Yard); there at the Green Court gate a monastery official, seneschal or porter, would inspect them. The poorer sort would mount by the Norman staircase to Strangers' Hall (also known as Hogs' Hall), now the library of the King's School. Those of better class would be conducted along a wooden covered way known still as the Pentise – half of which can still be seen in a school boarding-house garden – into the Cellarer's Hall (now the Archdeacon's house), where they occupied chambers called Paradise and Heaven, which can also be seen.

The most celebrated visitors of all lodged, however, at the east end of the cathedral – kings, princes, cardinals and such like. The Prior's Lodgings were then more extensive in this direction than now, but still there remains one majestic house where these distinguished folk ate and recreated themselves. For seven hundred years it has borne the name 'Meister Omers'. All the great folk were housed there, and you may still see the vast kitchen fireplace, the long gallery, the splendid fresco commemorating Elizabeth's visit and the arms of the Beauforts, Dukes of Somerset, who lived there for a long time.

Duty, devotion or policy dictated to every king of England, from Henry II's penance to the Dissolution by Henry VIII, visits and pilgrimages to Canterbury. But the most spectacular figure of the Middle Ages was Edward, the Black Prince. His earliest connection with Canterbury was at the age of three, when his

14

father (Edward III) and mother brought him in 1333. When in 1363 he wanted to marry his cousin Joan, the price of a Papal dispensation was the founding of a chantry chapel in the crypt. This chantry chapel is now used by the Huguenot congregation, for since the days of Elizabeth I the cathedral has shown hospitality to the French Protestants.

The Black Prince's will instructed that he should be buried in the Chapel of Our Lady Undercroft – still the loveliest in the cathedral – but popular opinion demanded the most honourable spot for the nation's darling. So on 29th September, 1376, he was buried on the south side of Becket's Shrine. Opposite Edward lies Henry IV, who was to overthrow the Black Prince's son, Richard II, and reign in his stead.

'When I was in England I saw St. Thomas's tomb all over bedecked with a vast number of jewels of an immense price . . . the holy man . . . would have been better pleased to have his tomb adorned with leaves and flowers.'

The words of Erasmus, the Dutch theologian who spread the spirit of the Reformation throughout Europe, were heartily endorsed by Dean Colet of St. Paul's when the two men visited Canterbury Cathedral in 1512. The veneration of relics and the offering of worldly goods to atone for sins was being questioned. Within 25 years, Henry VIII, for political and personal purposes, had dissolved and plundered the religious houses of England. In 1538 he declared Becket a traitor and rebel; the Shrine was desecrated and robbed of its wealth; strict orders were given that wherever existed a memorial of Becket in any place and in whatever shape it should be destroyed. So perished in England the cult of St. Thomas.

A century later, in the protesting zeal of the Civil War, ancient glass, statues, monuments, vestments and rich hangings perished.

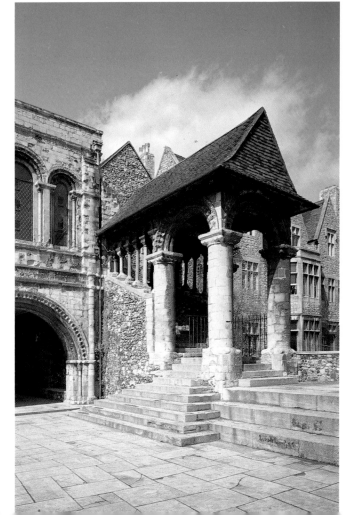

A link with the past is very much in evidence today in the Regimental Chapel of The Buffs, the Warriors' Chapel, where a page in the Book of Life is turned daily at 11 a.m. by a member of the Regimental Association. The Queen's Regiment was formed in 1966 through the amalgamation of various infantry regiments, including The Buffs, raised in 1572. Thousands of Canterbury men fought with The Buffs in the two World Wars and many other campaigns; they are commemorated each day at the service introduced by the ringing of the bell of HMS *Canterbury*.

Below left: ①
Font and font cover presented in 1639 by Bishop Warner of Rochester.

Top left: ⑬
Tomb of Archbishop Chichele (1414-43). His naked corpse is below his vestments.

Centre left: ㉙
A fine alabaster tomb showing Lady Margaret Holland (died 1439) flanked by her successive husbands, the Earl of Somerset (left) and the Duke of Clarence (right).

Below: ⑪
The north choir aisle showing the changeover from Norman to Gothic style.

Canterbury Cathedral attracts more visitors (about 2 million a year) now than it has ever done in its long history. Today's 'pilgrims' come to visit a great building where the echoes of history still resound and where important contemporary events still take place.

A plaque on the floor of the Martyrdom marks the spot where, on 29th May 1982, Pope John Paul II and the Archbishop of Canterbury, Dr Robert Runcie, knelt together in prayer. This was an important milestone along the long road of reconciliation between the Roman Catholic and Anglican Churches.

Another historic moment occurred on 13th February 1986 when the British Prime Minister, Mrs Margaret Thatcher, and President Mitterand of France signed the Visitors' Book together in the Huguenot Chapel after their agreement to proceed with the construction of the Channel Tunnel.

In the summer of 1988 Anglican bishops from all around the world converged on Canterbury for the Lambeth Conference. This ten-yearly gathering provides the Anglican Churches with an opportunity to worship together and to

discuss the major issues of the day. Each of the Churches in the Anglican Communion is independent, but together they accept the primacy of Canterbury.

Although the Archbishop of Canterbury has his seat, or *cathedra*, at Canterbury Cathedral, his official residence is at Lambeth Palace in London. The Cathedral itself is administered by the Dean and four Canons, assisted by a staff of about two hundred.

Amidst all the bustle and clamour, the reality of Canterbury Cathedral is that it was built as, and remains, a place in which to worship God.

Above: (21)
The Chapel of Saints and Martyrs of our own time, which used to be known as the Corona Chapel.

Left: (25)
Two of the four windows by Erwin Bossanyi, completed in 1960. The themes are Peace (left) and Salvation (right).

The nave looking east.